SPORTS GOATs: THE GREATEST OF ALL TIME

GOATs OF HOCKEY

BY ANTHONY K. HEWSON

An Imprint of Abdo Publishing
abdobooks.com

abdobooks.com

Published by Abdo Publishing, a division of ABDO, PO Box 398166, Minneapolis, Minnesota 55439.

Printed in the United States of America, North Mankato, Minnesota.
102021
012022

THIS BOOK CONTAINS RECYCLED MATERIALS

Cover Photo: Andy Martin Jr./Alamy
Interior Photos: Bettmann/Getty Images, 4, 4–5; AP Images, 6, 6–7, 12, 13; Pictorial Parade/Getty Images Sport/Getty Images, 8, 8–9; Denis Brodeur/National Hockey League/Getty Images, 10, 11, 14–15, 15; Ray Lussier/Boston Herald American/AP Images, 16, 16–17; Bruce Bennett Studios/Getty Images, 18, 18–19, 20–21, 21; IHA/Icon SMI/Icon Sportswire, 22–23, 23; Ron Frehm/AP Images, 24–25, 25; Gary Tramontina/AP Images, 26, 26–27; David Zalubowski/AP Images, 28, 28–29; Gene J. Puskar/AP Images, 30–31, 31, 40–41, 41; Paul Sancya/AP Images, 32, 32–33; Jeff Zelevansky/Icon SMI/Icon Sportswire, 34, 34–35; Ben Pelosse/QMI Agency/Zuma Press/Icon Sportswire, 36, 37; Nick Wass/AP Images, 38, 38–39; Alex Gallardo/AP Images, 42, 43

Editor: Charlie Beattie
Series Designer: Jake Nordby

Library of Congress Control Number: 2021941624

Publisher's Cataloging-in-Publication Data

Names: Hewson, Anthony K., author.
Title: GOATs of hockey / by Anthony K. Hewson
Description: Minneapolis, Minnesota : Abdo Publishing, 2022 | Series: Sports GOATs: The greatest of all time | Includes online resources and index.
Identifiers: ISBN 9781532196515 (lib. bdg.) | ISBN 9781644947111 (pbk.) | ISBN 9781098218324 (ebook)
Subjects: LCSH: Hockey--Juvenile literature. | Hockey players--Juvenile literature. | Hockey--Records--Juvenile literature. | Professional athletes--Juvenile literature.
Classification: DDC 796.962--dc23

TABLE OF CONTENTS

MAURICE RICHARD 4
TERRY SAWCHUK 6
DOUG HARVEY 8
GORDIE HOWE 10
JEAN BELIVEAU 12
BOBBY HULL 14
BOBBY ORR 16
MIKE BOSSY 18
WAYNE GRETZKY 20
RAY BOURQUE 22
MARK MESSIER 24
MARIO LEMIEUX 26
PATRICK ROY 28
JAROMIR JAGR 30
NICKLAS LIDSTROM 32
MARTIN BRODEUR 34
HAYLEY WICKENHEISER 36
ALEXANDER OVECHKIN 38
SIDNEY CROSBY 40
CONNOR MCDAVID 42

HONORABLE MENTIONS 44
GLOSSARY 46
MORE INFORMATION 47
ONLINE RESOURCES 47
INDEX 48
ABOUT THE AUTHOR 48

MAURICE RICHARD

Maurice Richard was working as a machinist making $40 per week before the Montreal Canadiens signed him in 1942. By the end of his career, he had scored at a pace no one had seen before.

Richard's career nearly didn't get started. He broke his ankle playing junior hockey in 1940. The next year he broke his wrist. In his rookie year in Montreal, he broke his leg and played only 16 games. Many wondered if the 5-foot-10-inch, 170-pound winger was too fragile.

His speed was built for the National Hockey League (NHL), however. With a lightning stride, the winger was a key part of the Canadiens' dominant "Punch Line." Defenders simply could not catch the man who would become known as "the Rocket." If they did hit him, they found he was tough enough to take the blow.

Richard became the NHL's first 50-goal scorer in 1944–45. He did it in just 50 games. He led the NHL in scoring five times in 18 seasons. And in 1957, Richard became the first player to score 500 career goals. Most importantly for Canadiens fans, he helped his team win eight Stanley Cups.

When he finally retired in 1960, he held nearly 20 NHL records. In 1999 the league created a new trophy for the highest goal scorer in a NHL season. Its name? The Maurice "Rocket" Richard Trophy.

FAST FACT

Alex Ovechkin is the only player to win more than two Richard Trophies. The legendary goal scorer won his ninth in 2020.

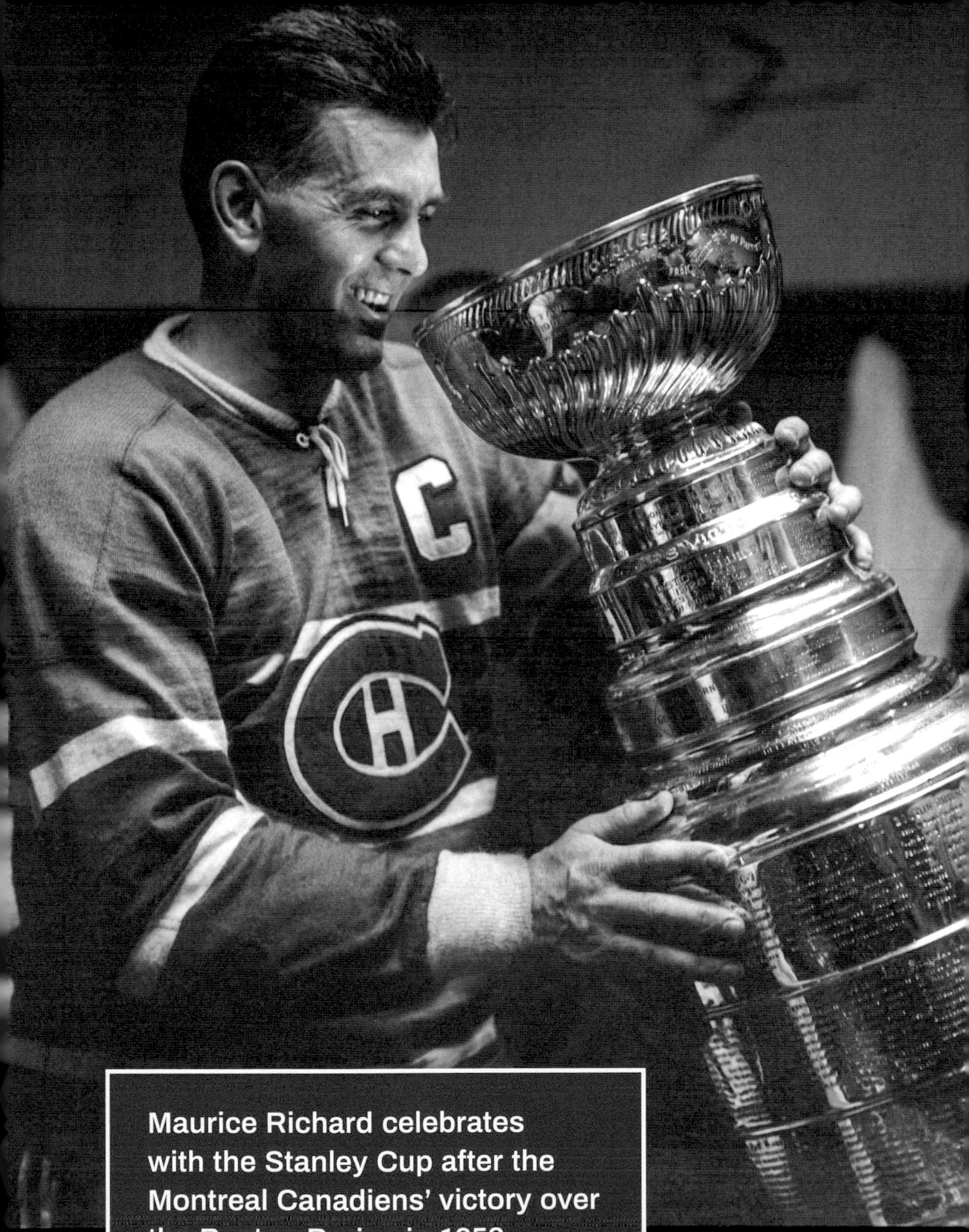

Maurice Richard celebrates with the Stanley Cup after the Montreal Canadiens' victory over the Boston Bruins in 1958.

TERRY SAWCHUK

It didn't take scouts long to see that Terry Sawchuk was going to be a special goaltender. Sawchuk was Rookie of the Year in two different minor leagues in 1948 and 1949. By 1949–50 he had earned a shot in the NHL.

Sawchuk played just seven games for the Detroit Red Wings that season. But he allowed only 16 goals, and he had one shutout. That was all Red Wings general manager Jack Adams needed to see. He traded starter Harry Lumley and gave the job to Sawchuk. It worked. Sawchuk won the Calder Trophy as NHL Rookie of the Year for 1950–51.

Sawchuk would guard an NHL net for the next 19 years. He played mostly with the Red Wings, but he also had stints with four other teams. Wherever he went, Sawchuk was a winner. He won 445 regular season games and 54 more in the playoffs, by far the most wins for a goalie at that time.

Sawchuk did all that winning in a difficult era for goaltenders. Goalies played more games and wore less safety equipment. Sawchuk suffered numerous broken bones. He also needed more than 400 stitches during his career. But he still played 60 games or more in eight different seasons.

Players typically must wait three years after retiring before being elected to the Hockey Hall of Fame. Sawchuk's wait was waived following his tragic death on May 31, 1970. He was elected to the hall the next season. For years after, he remained the standard for goalies.

Terry Sawchuk played much of his career before masks were standard for goalies.

DOUG HARVEY

Hockey came so easily to defenseman Doug Harvey that it sometimes looked like he wasn't working hard. His laid-back style had Montreal Canadiens fans booing him early in his career. He angered coaches by carrying the puck too long. They threatened to fine him every time a player stole the puck away and scored a goal as a result. But Harvey never had to pay a dime.

Sticking to his style made Harvey a star. The Norris Trophy for best NHL defenseman was created in 1954. It might as well have been named the Harvey Trophy. The Canadiens' standout won seven of the first nine awarded.

The Canadiens were known for their high-powered scoring attack. Harvey's steady presence on defense made everything possible. He controlled the puck and waited to make a perfect pass. The way he helped run the offense was unusual for defensemen at the time. This unique style helped him reach the 50-point mark in 1956–57.

Harvey was at his best when Montreal was on the power play. Until 1956 a power play didn't end when a goal was scored. With Harvey distributing the puck, Montreal was able to pile up multiple goals on each man advantage.

Harvey won his last Norris Trophy in 1962 while playing with the New York Rangers. He did it while also serving as the team's head coach. But Harvey will always be remembered as a Canadien. The team retired his No. 2 jersey in 1985.

Doug Harvey, *left,* of the Montreal Canadiens keeps his eye on the puck as he throws a heavy body check.

GORDIE HOWE

Gordie Howe had many nicknames. He was called "the Great Gordie," "the Legend," and even "Mr. Elbows" for his punishing hits. But to most fans, he will always be known simply as "Mr. Hockey." Even Wayne Gretzky, who would smash all of Howe's NHL records, considered Howe the greatest player ever.

Howe signed with the Detroit Red Wings in 1946. He played his final NHL game in 1980, when he was 52 years old. Howe's record of 1,767 games stood until 2021. That number could have been even higher. But Howe played in the World Hockey Association (WHA), a rival league to the NHL, for six seasons in the 1970s.

Wearing his famous No. 9 sweater, Howe did everything well. He was a smooth skater, a pinpoint passer, and a thumping checker. Along with teammates Sid Abel and Ted Lindsay, he formed Detroit's famous "Production Line." The three all-time greats were the top three NHL scorers in 1949–50. Howe did not slow down with age. He scored more than 100 points in a season three times in his career. All of them came after he turned 40 years old.

FAST FACT

In 1997 Howe suited up with the minor-league Detroit Vipers for one game. The appearance marked his sixth decade of pro hockey.

Howe won six Hart Trophy awards as the league's Most Valuable Player (MVP) and owned nearly every record when he retired. He scored 20 or more goals in 22 consecutive seasons. He scored 801 NHL goals and had 1,850 NHL points. He also tallied more than 500 points in the WHA.

Between his time in the NHL and WHA, Gordie Howe played in 2,186 professional regular-season games and 235 playoff games.

JEAN BELIVEAU

The Canadiens owned Jean Beliveau's rights in the early 1950s. If he wanted to play professional hockey, it had to be with Montreal. But Beliveau was a star in his local amateur league. He wasn't sure the NHL was right for him. The Canadiens came up with a solution. They bought the entire league and made it professional. Now he had to either sign with Montreal or stop playing hockey.

He signed and began a decorated 20-year career that included 10 Stanley Cup titles. The center added to an already dominant Montreal team that included Maurice Richard and Doug Harvey. Beliveau was a great skater, both fast and smooth. He could score or make a final pass for an open teammate.

Fans knew him as "Le Gros Bill," meaning "Big Bill" in French. Standing 6 feet, 3 inches tall and weighing 205 pounds, Beliveau could play physically when he needed to. Defenders struggled to figure out how to stop such a big and fast skater. But while Beliveau was a powerful player, he was also a gentleman of hockey. In 1961 Beliveau's teammates voted to make him captain. Beliveau was known for his leadership and good sportsmanship just as much as his goal scoring.

FAST FACT

Beliveau's name is on the Stanley Cup a record 17 times. His teammate Henri Richard holds the record for players with 11. In addition to Beliveau's 10 as a player, he added another seven while he was an executive for the Canadiens.

Beliveau played in 13 All-Star games and won two Hart Trophies. He won the first-ever Conn Smythe Trophy in 1965 as MVP of the playoffs. He is also remembered as one of the most dignified players ever. That showed when he was given the NHL's Lifetime Achievement Award—making him one of just two to receive that honor.

Jean Beliveau skates with his tenth, and final, Stanley Cup as a player after the Montreal Canadiens' victory in 1971.

In 1,474 games between the NHL and WHA, Bobby Hull scored 913 career regular-season goals.

BOBBY HULL

Everything about Bobby Hull seemed fast. The speedy forward was often seen as a blur skating down the ice. In an era where players did not always wear helmets, Hull's flowing blond hair earned him the nickname "the Golden Jet."

But Hull's legendary skating speed was only one aspect of his game. He owned an incredibly hard slap shot. Hull's shot routinely traveled 100 miles per hour (161 km/h) long before such speeds were common.

Hull was also quick to do things that hadn't been done before. Before Hull scored 50 goals in 1961–62, only two players in NHL history had done so in a season. Hull did it five times in 15 seasons with the Chicago Black Hawks, as they were known before changing the name to "Blackhawks" in 1986.

Hockey sticks hadn't changed much since they were invented in the 1830s. Hull and Hawks teammate Stan Mikita started experimenting with curved blades in the 1960s. The curved blades made it easier to handle the puck and to shoot harder. It worked so well that other players began copying the idea. Soon the NHL had to make rules about how much curve was allowed.

One of the first stars to leave the NHL for the WHA, Hull spent seven seasons in the rival league with the Winnipeg Jets. He scored more than 300 goals in that span before returning to the NHL for his final season in 1980. He left the NHL with 610 goals, third most of any player at the time. Statues of both Hull and Mikita stand outside the Blackhawks' home rink in Chicago.

BOBBY ORR

In Boston he's simply known as "No. 4" for his famous jersey. Bobby Orr was not the first defenseman who could score. But he was the first one who could score like a forward. Orr changed how defensemen played forever.

In 1969–70, his fourth season with the Boston Bruins, Orr led the NHL in assists and finished with a league-best 120 points. It was the first time a defenseman had led the NHL in scoring. Orr went on to do it four more times. No defenseman did it again until Erik Karlsson during the 2015–16 season.

The 1969–70 season was also the year Orr won the Hart Trophy for the first time. He won three in a row, which had never been done before. Orr wasn't just a scorer who happened to play defense. He was an eight-time winner of the Norris Trophy for best defenseman.

Orr's historic 1969–70 season ended in iconic fashion. In the moment after he scored the goal that won the Bruins the Stanley Cup, Orr was tripped. A photo captured Orr flying through the air. It became one of the most famous images in sports history. The image was also turned into a statue, which sits outside the Bruins' home arena.

Orr played with great speed and stick handling ability. The only thing that could slow him down was injury. Orr dealt with knee problems throughout his career. He won his eighth Norris Trophy in 1974–75, but he played just 36 games over the next three seasons. He retired in 1979 at the age of 30. But his playing style left a lasting influence on the game.

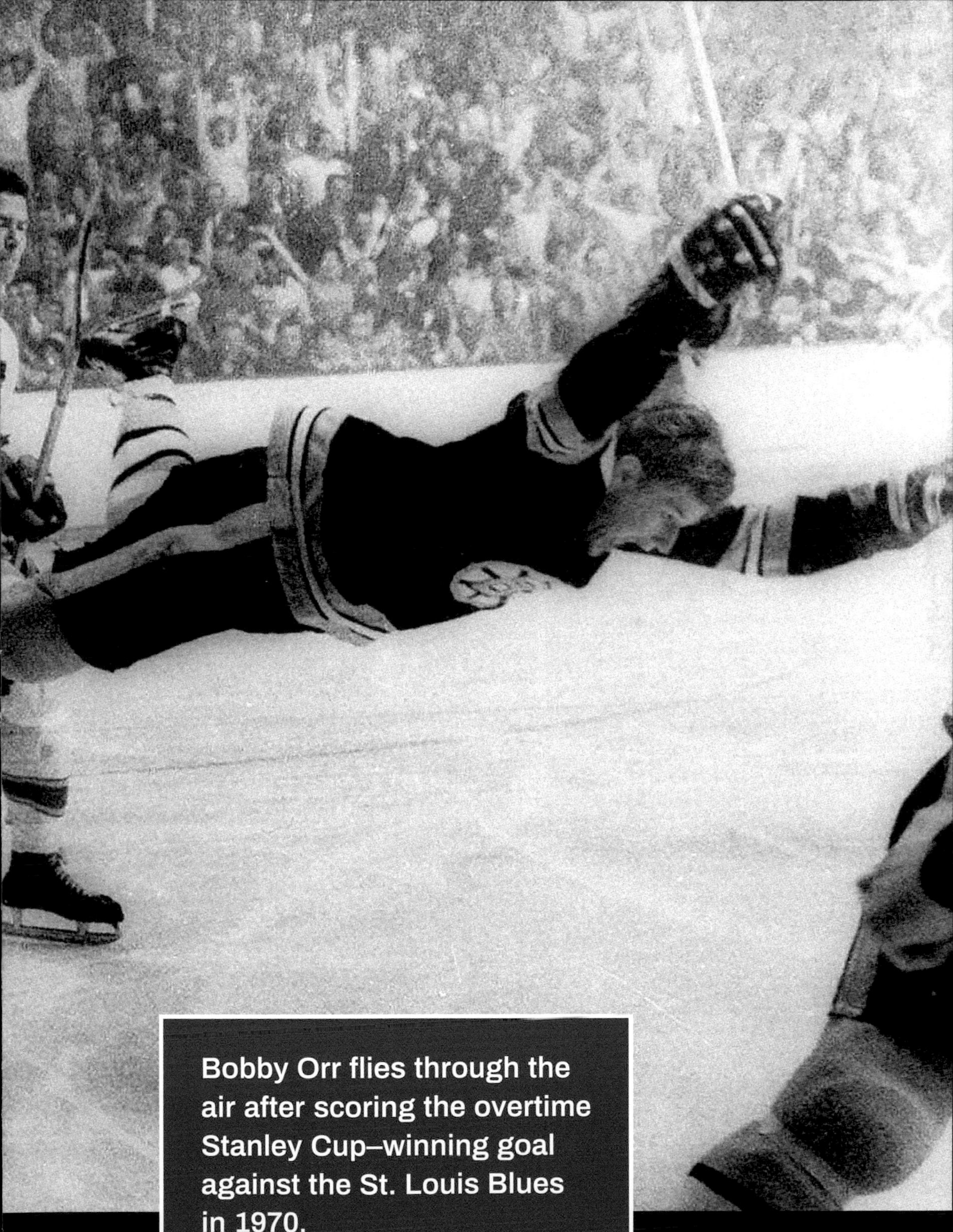

Bobby Orr flies through the air after scoring the overtime Stanley Cup–winning goal against the St. Louis Blues in 1970.

MIKE BOSSY

Fewer than 50 players have scored 500 career NHL goals. Only three of them reached that total in fewer than 1,000 games played. Maurice Richard did it in 978 career games. Mario Lemieux needed 915 games. Winger Mike Bossy's 573 career goals came in only 752 appearances in a New York Islanders uniform. Had injuries not slowed Bossy down, he would certainly be the greatest goal scorer the NHL has ever seen.

Bossy was a star from the moment he put on an Islanders sweater in 1977. He scored in his first game and finished the year with 53 goals. That was a rookie record at the time.

With speed and quick hands, Bossy was too much for NHL teams to handle over the next decade. His 50-plus goals in each of his first nine seasons set a NHL record.

Bossy didn't just score. He also won Stanley Cups. The Islanders won four straight championships from 1980 to 1983, and Bossy scored 61 postseason goals during that stretch. He even scored the Stanley Cup-clinching goals in both the 1982 and 1983 finals.

Back injuries hampered Bossy's career. The 1978–79 season was his only year playing every game. In 1986–87 he was limited to 63 games. That year he failed to score 50 goals, though he still managed 38. After sitting out the 1987–88 season to rest his back, Bossy wanted to play again. But he was never able to. He retired averaging .762 goals per game, the highest rate in NHL history.

Mike Bossy scored 80 career game-winning goals in just 752 regular-season games. He added 17 more in 129 playoff games.

FAST FACT

Gordie Howe established the record for NHL points over the course of 25 seasons. Gretzky needed only 10 seasons to pass Howe's mark. He spent the next 10 years adding to his amazing totals.

WAYNE GRETZKY

Great players established NHL records in the 1950s, '60s, and '70s. In the 1980s and '90s, Wayne Gretzky smashed them all. In recognition his No. 99 has been retired by every team in the league.

The signs he would become "the Great One" were there from the very beginning. Gretzky started skating at the age of two. His father Walter provided coaching on the frozen rink in the family's Ontario backyard. His guiding advice to Wayne was to skate to where the puck is going, not where it was.

At the age of six, Gretzky was playing with 10-year-olds. At nine a newspaper compared him to Gordie Howe, Maurice Richard, and Bobby Hull. At age 10, he reportedly scored 382 goals in 82 games.

After a year in the WHA in 1978–79, Gretzky moved to the NHL when his team, the Edmonton Oilers, switched leagues. The young center was an instant hit, winning the Hart Trophy and leading the NHL in scoring his first season. That started a streak of eight consecutive scoring titles. In 1981–82 he established the NHL single-season goals record with 92. Gretzky recorded 200 points in a season four times. Nobody else has done it even once.

After stops with the Los Angeles Kings, St. Louis Blues, and New York Rangers, Gretzky retired in 1999. He held nearly every major offensive record in the book, including 894 total goals and 1,963 assists. His 2,857 career points are over 900 more than any other player.

Wayne Gretzky holds up the Stanley Cup after his Edmonton Oilers defeated the Philadelphia Flyers in the 1987 finals.

Ray Bourque of the Boston Bruins circles the net during a 1998 game.

RAY BOURQUE

No one will ever make Bruins fans forget Bobby Orr. But just a few years after Orr left the team, Ray Bourque arrived to fill Orr's skates on Boston's blue line.

Bourque made his Bruins debut in 1979. And he was a star from day one. He scored a goal in his first game and finished the season with 17 goals and 48 assists. That earned him the Calder Trophy for Rookie of the Year. Known for his offense, Bourque became the NHL's all-time leader among defensemen in goals (410), assists (1,169), and total points (1,579).

Bourque was just as strong on defense. In 20 seasons in Boston, Bourque won the Norris Trophy five times. Only Orr, Doug Harvey, and Nicklas Lidstrom have won the award more times.

Bourque spent parts of 21 seasons with the Bruins before being traded in March of 2000. In 1985 he became the team captain. He held the post for 15 years, longer than any other Boston player.

By 2000 there was just one thing missing from Bourque's career. He and the Bruins had come close to winning the Stanley Cup earlier in his career but never could do it. The Bruins were no longer contenders, so he asked to be traded to a team that could win it all. The Bruins agreed, and Bourque was sent to the Colorado Avalanche.

Even at the age of 40, Bourque showed he had plenty left the next season as he scored 59 points in 2000–01. And at the end of the year, Bourque was finally able to lift the Stanley Cup. Colorado defeated the New Jersey Devils in seven games for the title. It was a crowning achievement for one of the greatest defensemen ever.

Mark Messier scores one of his three goals in game six of the 1994 Eastern Conference Finals against the New Jersey Devils. Messier's Rangers won 4–2 after he had guaranteed a victory.

MARK MESSIER

Mark Messier could do it all. He was a great skater and defender who could score goals and play a physical game. But the center was best known for being one of the NHL's great leaders. He was the first player to serve as captain on two different Stanley Cup–winning teams.

Messier formed a dynamic duo with Wayne Gretzky while playing with the Edmonton Oilers. Gretzky grabbed most of the headlines. But Messier took a starring role in the 1984 playoffs, winning the Conn Smythe Trophy as the Oilers won their first Stanley Cup. He would win five more Stanley Cups in his career.

Some fans believed the Oilers would fade after Gretzky was traded in the summer of 1988. But Messier took over as captain, and Edmonton stayed on top. Messier had 31 points in the playoffs, as the Oilers won another Stanley Cup in 1990. He also won his first of two Hart Trophies that season.

Messier cemented his legacy as a great leader after moving to the New York Rangers in 1991. With the Rangers facing elimination in Game 6 of the 1994 Eastern Conference Finals, Messier guaranteed a Rangers victory. He then scored a hat trick to back up his promise. Soon after, he led the team to its first Stanley Cup in 54 years.

After a 25-year NHL career, Messier retired in 2004 as the NHL's second-leading scorer. Following the 2006–07 season, the NHL created the Mark Messier Leadership Award for players who set a positive example on and off the ice.

MARIO LEMIEUX

If scientists were to design a perfect hockey player, the result would look a lot like Mario Lemieux. He had the size, standing 6 feet, 4 inches tall before he even put skates on. He had the speed to burst through the defense. And he had the stickhandling to make goalies look silly. It all added up to the total package.

Lemieux debuted as a center with the Pittsburgh Penguins in 1984–85 with a 100-point season. It quickly became clear that he was the only player who could challenge Wayne Gretzky's scoring totals. One of the two led the NHL in scoring every year from 1979–80 through 1993–94.

Lemieux came very close to joining Gretzky in the 200-point club in 1988–89, finishing with 199 points. On three occasions, he tallied eight points in a single game, including one in the playoffs. Gretzky only had two eight-point games in his entire career. That year Lemieux won his second of six Art Ross Trophies, given to the league's top scorer.

Injuries and illness began to take a toll on Lemieux. Back problems forced him to miss 21 games the next season and 50 games in 1990–91. He was diagnosed with cancer during the 1992–93 season and played only 60 games. But he still won the Hart Trophy. After retiring in April 1997, he came back in December 2000 to play five more seasons.

Lemieux played in just 915 career games. But he racked up more than 1,700 career points. Fans can only wonder how high those numbers would have gone if he had been healthy throughout his career.

FAST FACT

uring his first retirement
1999, Lemieux became
wner of the Penguins.
hat made him the first
erson in the history of
orth American pro sports
own the team he once
layed for.

Mario Lemieux makes a move during a game in 1996. He finished the season with an NHL-best 122 points.

PATRICK ROY

Few stars can say they changed the way their position is played. Patrick Roy is one of them. Before Roy made his NHL debut in 1985, goalies made most of their saves while standing upright. Roy helped popularize a style in which goalies dropped to their knees to stop shots. This became known as the butterfly style.

Nothing would have changed if Roy were not successful. He began his career with the Montreal Canadiens and finished it with the Colorado Avalanche. He won 200 games for each team. He won the Vezina Trophy for best goaltender three times. And Roy did it all with flash and fiery competitiveness.

Roy was great in the regular season. He was even better in the playoffs. He retired in 2003 having won 151 playoff games in his career. That was the most in history. Roy was a key player in four Stanley Cup wins. He won the Conn Smythe Trophy as playoff MVP three times. That was the most for any player.

In 2008 Roy became the sixth player in NHL history to have his number retired by two teams. His No. 33 will never be worn by any other player for the Canadiens or the Avalanche. He later went into coaching, even returning as head coach in Colorado from the 2013–14 season through 2015–16.

FAST FACT

In addition to his three Vezina Trophies, Roy won the Jennings Trophy five times. The award is given to any goaltender who plays at least 25 games for the team that allows the fewest goals in a season.

Patrick Roy drops down to stop a shot in 2002, his final season in the NHL.

Jaromir Jagr battles for a puck while playing for the Pittsburgh Penguins in November 1998. Jagr finished the season with a career-high 127 points.

JAROMIR JAGR

In the mid-1990s, Wayne Gretzky's career was winding down. Mario Lemieux was battling injuries and illness. The NHL needed new scoring stars to step up. Winger Jaromir Jagr, Lemieux's teammate in Pittsburgh, was ready to take over.

Born in Czechoslovakia (now the Czech Republic), he made his NHL debut in October 1990. At 18 years old, he was the youngest player in the league. With Lemieux and Jagr leading the way, the Penguins won the Stanley Cup in each of the winger's first two seasons.

He would never win another championship. But Jagr did add many individual honors. He won five Art Ross Trophies. Four of those titles came in four straight years from 1997–98 to 2000–01. He was also the Hart Trophy winner as league MVP in 1998–99.

Although Jagr left the Penguins in 2001, his time in the NHL was far from over. He suited up for nine teams in his 24 seasons. His last game in the NHL came in 2017, when he was 45. He was just 35 games away from breaking Gordie Howe's all-time record for games played.

Jagr owned many other NHL marks. His 149 points in the 1995–96 season were the most ever by a European-born player. At age 42, he became the oldest player to record an NHL hat trick. When he retired, his 1,921 points ranked second of all time.

Just because he left the NHL, it didn't mean Jagr was done. In 2021 he was still playing in his home city of Kladno, Czech Republic. It was his thirty-third season of professional hockey.

NICKLAS LIDSTROM

Detroit Red Wings goalie Chris Osgood and forward Kris Draper needed a nickname for their beloved teammate, defenseman Nicklas Lidstrom. They decided on "the Perfect Human."

It was easy to see why. The Swedish-born Lidstrom seemed to do everything well. His Red Wings teams were rarely scored on when he was on the ice. Lidstrom almost never threw body checks. He didn't need to. Instead he patrolled his defensive zone with expert positioning and stick work. And he could score too. Lidstrom's 264 goals ranked him eighth of all time among all NHL defensemen.

His career was also nearly perfect. In 20 NHL seasons, he missed only 44 games. The Red Wings never missed the playoffs in his career. When he joined in 1991, the team had not won a Stanley Cup since 1955. Five seasons later, he helped end that streak. It was the first of his four titles with the Red Wings. Lidstrom's playoff peak came in 2002 when he was named the Conn Smythe Trophy winner after scoring 16 points in 23 games.

After longtime Red Wings captain Steve Yzerman retired in 2006, Lidstrom was quickly named captain in his place. He was 36 at the time but still far from done. As team captain, he was the first to lift Detroit's Stanley Cup trophy in 2008. And he won three of his seven Norris Trophies as the NHL's best defenseman after donning the *C* on his sweater. Only Bobby Orr, with eight, won more Norris Trophies than "the Perfect Human."

Nicklas Lidstrom unleashes a shot during a game with the Calgary Flames in November 2006.

MARTIN BRODEUR

Many considered Terry Sawchuk's record of 103 career shutouts to be unbreakable. It would take more than three decades before anyone even challenged it. That player was Martin Brodeur. And he set plenty of other records too.

Brodeur debuted in March 1991 with the New Jersey Devils. Even back then, he was considered a throwback. At the time most goalies were copying Patrick Roy's butterfly. Brodeur, on the other hand, played more of the old stand-up style. His goaltending technique would change slightly in his career. But standing worked well for the Montreal native.

In an era when starting goalies started taking more games off, Brodeur was almost a constant in net for the Devils. He played 70 games or more in each of 12 different seasons. In the 2006–07 season, his backup started only four times. In addition, Brodeur steadily improved in his early years. By 1996–97 he led the league in goals-against average and shutouts.

It took Brodeur until 2003 to win his first Vezina Trophy. Then he won four in five seasons. In 2009 he broke Roy's record for total wins with his 552nd. And on December 21, 2009, Brodeur turned away 35 Pittsburgh Penguin shots to finally break Sawchuk's shutout record.

Brodeur played until 2015. When he retired, his records stood at 691 wins and 125 shutouts. At the end of the 2021 season, no active goaltender had reached even 500 wins. And no active goaltender had more than 67 shutouts.

Martin Brodeur snags a shot during a 2003 playoff game. Brodeur posted seven shutouts in 24 postseason games that year as he led the New Jersey Devils to a Stanley Cup victory.

HAYLEY WICKENHEISER

Women's hockey started to take root in Canada and the United States in the 1980s. By the mid-1990s, stars were beginning to emerge. Canada's Hayley Wickenheiser would play that starring role for the next two decades.

It didn't matter to Wickenheiser who she played against. She just wanted to play at the highest level she could. That meant skating with boys until she was 12. She regularly suited up against older girls too.

It didn't take long for Wickenheiser to get noticed. At age 15, she was called up to the Canadian national team for the 1994 World Championships. Wickenheiser would play a key role on the team for the next 23 years.

Wickenheiser became the greatest player for the sport's most dominant national team. She won four Olympic gold medals and seven World Championships. She scored 168 goals and had 379 points in 276 career international games. That easily made her Canada's all-time top scorer.

Shortly after winning Canada's first Olympic gold medal in women's hockey in 2002, Wickenheiser sought to challenge herself. She signed with a men's professional team in Finland. With two goals and

FAST FACT

In 1992 Canadian goalie Manon Rheaume appeared in a preseason game for the Tampa Bay Lightning. That made her the first woman to play in a major North American pro sports league.

10 assists, she became the first woman to score a point in a men's pro league. Wickenheiser later played part of another season in Finland.

After retiring in 2017, Wickenheiser earned a medical degree. She also became an executive for the Toronto Maple Leafs. In 2019 she became the seventh woman ever inducted into the Hockey Hall of Fame.

Hayley Wickenheiser celebrates a goal for Team Canada against Switzerland during the 2014 Olympics in Sochi, Russia.

ALEXANDER OVECHKIN

Alex Ovechkin turned 18 years old two days late to be eligible for the 2003 NHL Draft. The Florida Panthers wanted to choose him so badly that they tried to argue that if leap years were counted, Ovechkin would already be 18. That didn't work. The Panthers missed out, and the Washington Capitals were the lucky ones to select the winger first overall in 2004.

Still a teenager, "Ovie" made his debut in October 2005. That season he had 106 points and was Rookie of the Year. Points kept coming for the young Russian. He proved to be one of the league's most talented goal scorers right away. Many of his goals were incredible highlights.

Ovechkin was a big, powerful skater. But he had a way of sneaking through small spaces to get in place for a shot. His powerful slap shot was incredibly accurate. Goalies had to be perfect to react in time.

Ovechkin was also durable. In his first 15 seasons, only two players in the NHL played more games. Ovechkin's goal totals soared as a result. In 2020 he scored the 700th of his career. Even at the age of 34, he was still going strong.

The 2019–20 season ended with Ovechkin winning his ninth goal-scoring title. In 2021 he moved into sixth place of all time with his 718th career goal. He finished the season with 730. Some fans wondered if he would be able to challenge Wayne Gretzky's all-time record of 894.

Alex Ovechkin fires off a one-time slap shot while playing for the Washington Capitals. His shot has been measured as high as 101.3 miles per hour (163.0 km/h).

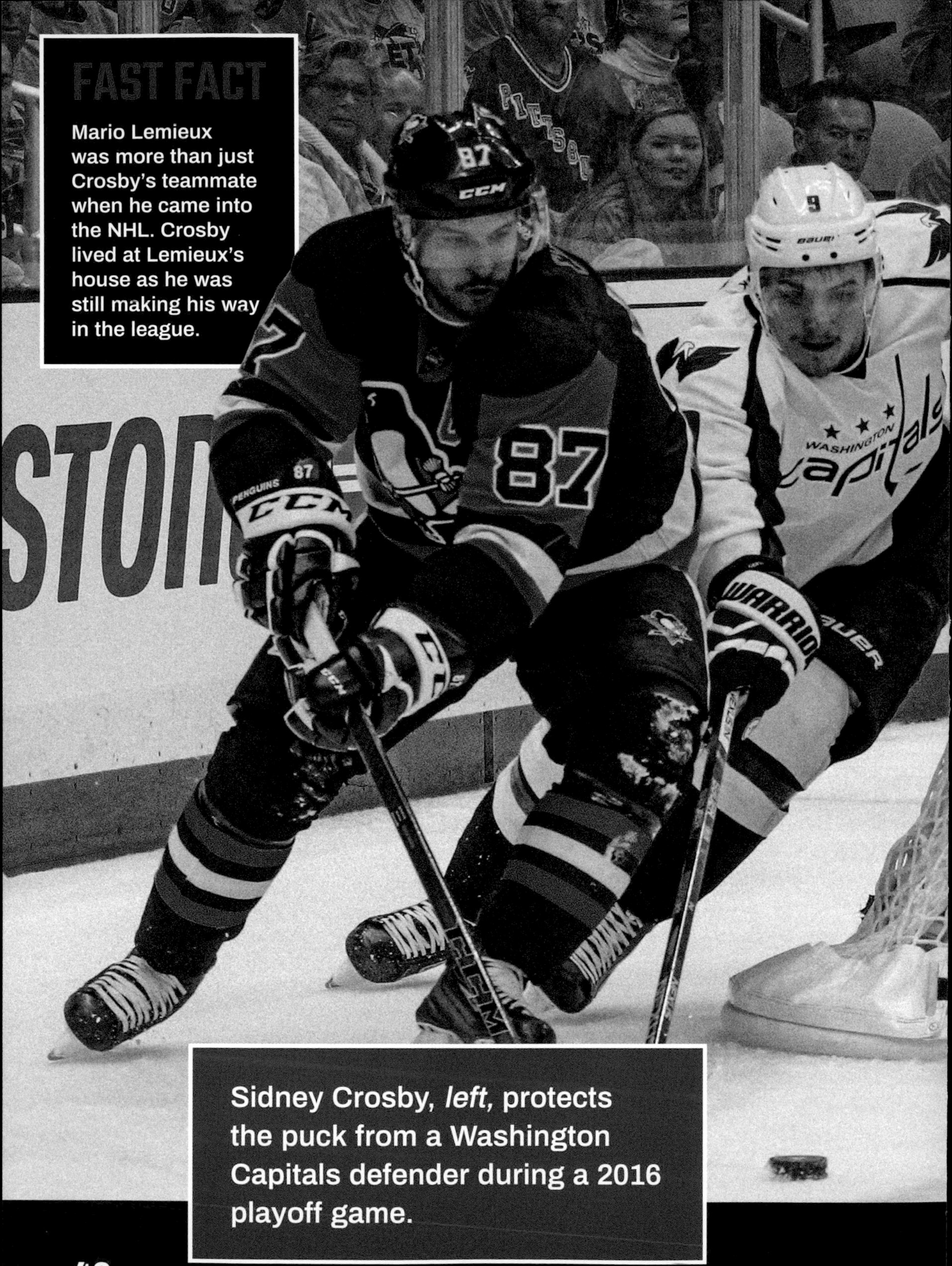

FAST FACT

Mario Lemieux was more than just Crosby's teammate when he came into the NHL. Crosby lived at Lemieux's house as he was still making his way in the league.

Sidney Crosby, *left*, protects the puck from a Washington Capitals defender during a 2016 playoff game.

SIDNEY CROSBY

If Wayne Gretzky was "the Great One," then Sidney Crosby was "the Next One." Instead of a backyard rink, Crosby honed his shooting skills in the family laundry room. If he missed the net, he would put a dent in the clothes dryer.

Crosby's scoring ability was legendary even as a teenager. He played two seasons for Rimouski of the Quebec Major Junior Hockey League before being drafted. In a span of 121 regular-season games, Crosby put up 303 points.

Fans could not wait to see him in the NHL. The Pittsburgh Penguins got him first overall in the 2005 draft. Playing with the legendary Mario Lemieux, Crosby looked like a fitting successor. His game translated to the NHL right away. Crosby had 102 points in his rookie season and led the league with 120 his second year. That season he won his first Hart Trophy.

In addition to scoring, he was known for his all-around game. A powerful skating center, Crosby defended well. A leader on the ice, he was named captain of the Penguins when he was just 20 years old. He went on to lead the team to three Stanley Cups in 16 years.

Success didn't always come easy. Crosby dealt with concussion issues and a broken jaw that limited him to 99 games from the 2010–11 through 2012–13 seasons. But he rebounded in 2013–14 to lead the league in points once again and won a second Art Ross Trophy.

In 2017 the NHL celebrated its 100th anniversary by naming its top 100 players of all time. Crosby was one of just six active players chosen for the list.

CONNOR MCDAVID

Much like Sidney Crosby and Wayne Gretzky before him, Connor McDavid was hyped as a future star from a very young age. And like the two legends, McDavid lived up to the attention.

After scoring 285 points in three years of junior hockey, McDavid was taken first overall in 2015 by the Edmonton Oilers. A broken collarbone limited McDavid to just 45 games his first season. But he wowed fans with 48 points. He was named the Oilers team captain that summer. Still a teenager, McDavid was the youngest permanent captain in NHL history.

Teams struggled to defend his combination of speed and quick hands. McDavid's goals quickly became must-see highlights for NHL fans. In addition, McDavid's scoring pace placed him among some of the league's greatest players. In 2016–17 he became the third-youngest player ever to win a scoring title. Only Crosby and Gretzky did it at a younger age.

Despite playing only 56 games during the shortened 2020–21 season, McDavid still finished with 105 points. Nobody had posted 100 points in 56 or fewer games since Mario Lemieux and Jaromir Jagr

FAST FACT

At the NHL's annual fastest skater competition, McDavid became the first to win three in a row from 2017 to 2019. In 2017 McDavid did his lap of the rink in a career-best 13.310 seconds.

in 1995–96. McDavid became the third active player with four 100-point seasons by age 25. Crosby and Alex Ovechkin were the others.

McDavid had quickly established himself as one of the best players in the world. And he was already among hockey's greatest players ever. Only time would tell how far he could climb.

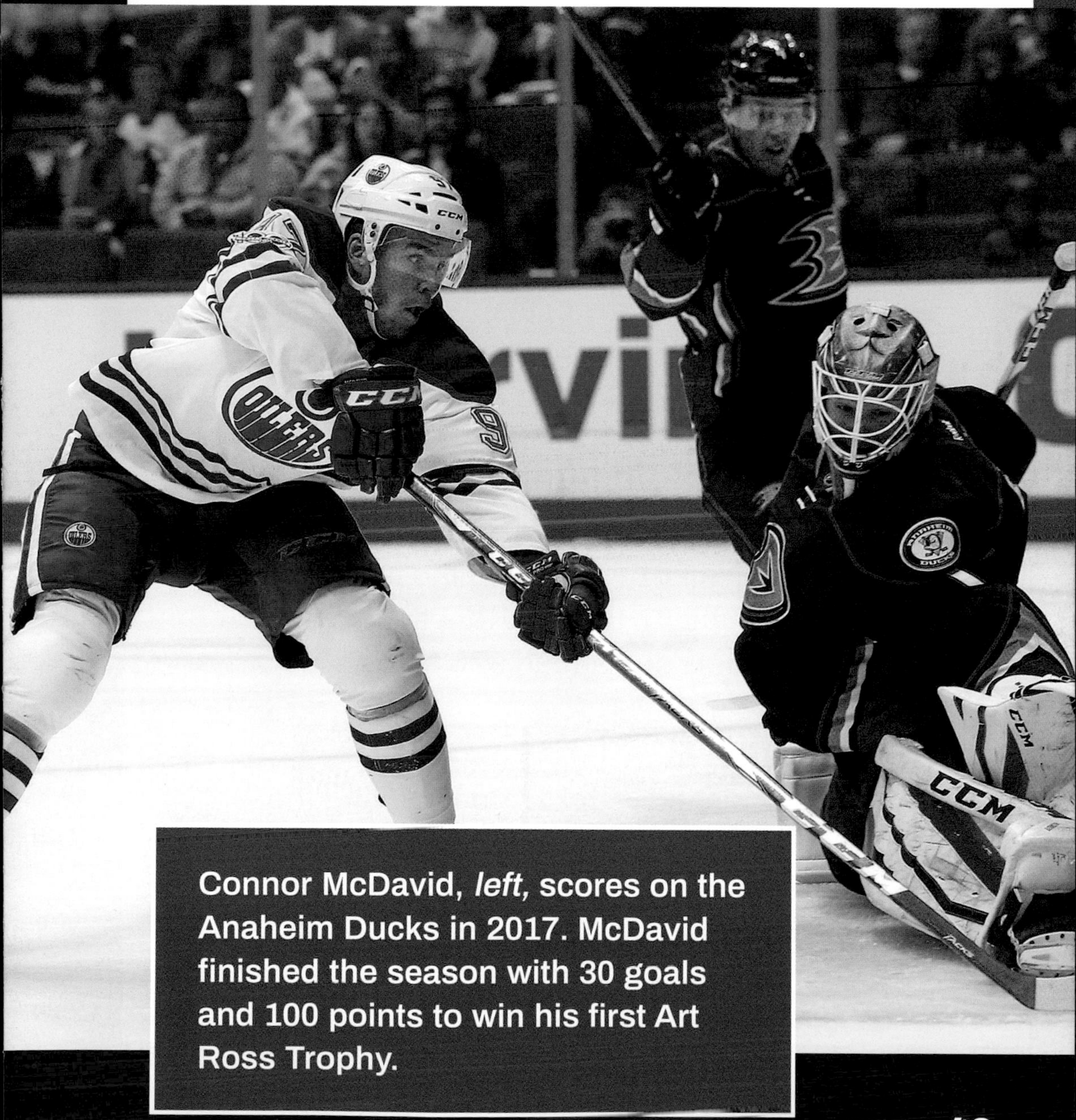

Connor McDavid, *left,* scores on the Anaheim Ducks in 2017. McDavid finished the season with 30 goals and 100 points to win his first Art Ross Trophy.

HONORABLE MENTIONS

HOWIE MORENZ

One of the fastest players in the early NHL, Morenz had true end-to-end speed that thrilled Montreal Canadiens fans in the 1920s and '30s.

EDDIE SHORE

One of the biggest stars of the early days of the NHL, the defenseman won the Hart Trophy four times between 1926–27 and 1939–40.

STAN MIKITA

A durable and reliable forward for the Chicago Black Hawks, Mikita was one of the top playmakers in the NHL from 1959 to 1979. He scored 541 goals and added 926 assists.

PHIL ESPOSITO

The center finished with 717 goals during the 1960s and '70s. Esposito won two Hart Trophies and held the single-season goals record before Wayne Gretzky broke it.

GUY LAFLEUR

The first player to have 50 goals and 100 points for six seasons in a row, Lafleur led the Canadiens to five Stanley Cups in the 1970s.

DENIS POTVIN

The first NHL defenseman to score 1,000 career points, Potvin was a major part of the New York Islanders teams that won four consecutive Stanley Cups from 1980 to 1983.

STEVE YZERMAN

The longest-serving captain in NHL history, Yzerman manned center for the Detroit Red Wings from 1983 to 2006. Yzerman was a tough two-way forward who led the Red Wings to three Stanley Cup titles.

CAMMI GRANATO

Granato captained the US national team to gold at the Olympic debut of women's hockey in 1998. She is also the all-time leading US scorer and played in every women's world championship from 1990 to 2005.

GLOSSARY

amateur

A person who plays a sport without getting paid.

assists

Passes or shots that set up a teammate to score a goal.

captain

The team leader and the only player allowed to speak to game officials regarding the rules.

concussion

An injury caused by a severe blow to the head.

debut

First appearance.

draft

A system that allows teams to acquire new players coming into a league.

durable

Tough and long-lasting.

general manager

An executive who runs a team and is responsible for finding and signing players.

goals-against average

A statistic that tracks the number of goals a goalie gives up per game.

junior

A top level of amateur hockey.

power play

When one team has more players on the ice than the opponent because of a penalty by the opponent.

rookie

A professional athlete in his or her first year of competition.

slap shot

A hard and fast shot with a long backswing and powerful follow-through.

MORE INFORMATION

BOOKS

Davidson, B. Keith. *NHL*. New York: Crabtree Publishing, 2022.

Hewson, Anthony K. *US Women's Hockey Team*. Minneapolis, MN: Abdo Publishing, 2019.

Kortemeier, Todd. *Total Hockey*. Minneapolis, MN: Abdo Publishing, 2017.

ONLINE RESOURCES

To learn more about the GOATs of hockey, please visit **abdobooklinks.com** or scan this QR code. These links are routinely monitored and updated to provide the most current information available.

INDEX

Abel, Sid, 10
Adams, Jack, 6
Art Ross Trophy, 26, 41, 43

Beliveau, Jean, 12, 13
Bossy, Mike, 18, 19
Bourque, Ray, 22, 23
Brodeur, Martin, 34, 35

Calder Trophy, 6, 23
Conn Smythe Trophy, 3, 25, 28, 32
Crosby, Sidney, 40, 41, 42–43

Draper, Kris, 32

Gretzky, Walter, 21
Gretzky, Wayne, 10, 20, 21, 25, 26, 31, 38, 41, 42

Hart Trophy, 11, 13, 16, 21, 25, 26, 31, 41
Harvey, Doug, 8, 9, 12, 23
Howe, Gordie, 10, 11, 20, 21, 31
Hull, Bobby, 14, 15, 21

Jagr, Jaromir, 30–31, 42
Jennings Trophy, 28

Karlsson, Erik, 16

Lemieux, Mario, 18, 26, 27, 31, 40, 41, 42
Lidstrom, Nicklas, 23, 32, 33
Lindsay, Ted, 10
Lumley, Harry, 6

McDavid, Connor, 42, 43
Messier, Mark, 24, 25
Mikita, Stan, 15

Norris Trophy, 8, 16, 23, 32

Orr, Bobby, 16, 17, 23, 32
Osgood, Chris, 32
Ovechkin, Alex, 4, 38, 39, 43

Rheaume, Manon, 36
Richard, Henri, 12
Richard, Maurice, 4–5, 12, 18, 21
  trophy, 4

Sawchuk, Terry, 6, 7, 34
Stanley Cup, 4, 5, 12–13, 16–19, 23, 25, 28, 31–32, 35, 41

Wickenheiser, Hayley, 36, 37

Yzerman, Steve, 32

ABOUT THE AUTHOR

Anthony K. Hewson is a freelance writer originally from San Diego. He and his wife now live in the San Francisco Bay Area with their two dogs.